Contents

KU-507-080

Some words are printed in bold, **like this**. You can find out what they mean by looking in the glossary.

Introducing Algeria

Have you ever read about or seen pictures of Algeria? What do you know about this large African country? If you imagine a vast, hot, desert landscape, you are on the right track. About four times the size of Spain, Algeria's land is over 80 per cent desert. The Sahara Desert covers most of North Africa, including Algeria and its neighbouring countries.

However, very few Algerians live in the sun-baked desert. Algeria also has a beautiful coastline where the land meets the Mediterranean Sea. Most Algerians live near this coast. Here, farms are abundant and large cities have modern services such as satellite television and access to the internet.

Although people have lived in the region since ancient times, Algeria was established as an independent country just 50 years ago. Since its **independence**, Algeria has had problems such as unhealthy water, too few houses, and even civil war. In this same period of time, the country has made strong progress in providing education and healthcare to its people. Algeria's government has also become a leader for peace and **trade** in North Africa.

In the midst of both problems and growth, Algeria's people maintain strong traditions. Family ties are very important. Religious beliefs guide everyday actions as well as major decisions. Music expresses wise sayings, religious ideas, and strong emotions. With a rich history and deep values, Algerians are proud of their land and **heritage**.

Recent unrest

Recently, Algeria has experienced **unrest** in its cities. In early 2011, groups of angry Algerians gathered to publicly complain about high food prices, lack of freedoms, and dishonesty among leaders. Many Algerians hope the unrest will lead to positive changes in the government.

B53 045 339 0

Countries Around the World

Algeria

WITHDRAWN
FROM THE
ROTHERHAM
PUBLIC
LIBRARY

This

The
a fu

Lori McManus

www.raintreepublishers.co.uk
Visit our website to find out more information about Raintree books.

To order:

☎ Phone 0845 6044371

🖷 Fax +44 (0) 1865 312263

🖥 Email myorders@raintreepublishers.co.uk

Customers from outside the UK please telephone +44 1865 312262

Raintree is an imprint of Capstone Global Library Limited, a company incorporated in England and Wales having its registered office at 7 Pilgrim Street, London, EC4V 6LB – Registered company number: 6695582

Text © Capstone Global Library Limited 2012
First published in hardback in 2012
Paperback edition first published in 2013
The moral rights of the proprietor have been asserted.

All rights reserved. No part of this publication may be reproduced in any form or by any means (including photocopying or storing it in any medium by electronic means and whether or not transiently or incidentally to some other use of this publication) without the written permission of the copyright owner, except in accordance with the provisions of the Copyright, Designs and Patents Act 1988 or under the terms of a licence issued by the Copyright Licensing Agency, Saffron House, 6–10 Kirby Street, London EC1N 8TS (www.cla.co.uk). Applications for the copyright owner's written permission should be addressed to the publisher.

Edited by Abby Colich and Megan Cotugno
Designed by Philippa Jenkins
Original illustrations © Capstone Global Library Ltd 2012
Illustrated by Oxford Designers & Illustrators
Picture research by Liz Alexander
Originated by Capstone Global Library Ltd
Printed in China by CTPS

ISBN 978 1 406 23561 6 (hardback)
16 15 14 13 12
10 9 8 7 6 5 4 3 2 1

ISBN 978 1 406 23568 5 (paperback)
17 16 15 14 13 12
10 9 8 7 6 5 4 3 2 1

British Library Cataloguing in Publication Data
McManus, Lori.
   Algeria. -- (Countries around the world)
   965'.054-dc22
A full catalogue record for this book is available from the British Library.

Acknowledgements
We would like to thank the following for permission to reproduce photographs: Alamy: pp. 15 (© imagebroker), 30 (© vario images GmbH & Co.KG), 31 (© Robert Harding Picture Library Ltd); Corbis: pp. 7 bottom (© Owen Franken), 25 (© Dani Cardona/Reuters), 35 (© Pascal Parrot/Sygma); Dreamstime.com: pp. 7 top (© Carolecastelli), 20 (© Dmitry Pichugin), 26 main (© Paul Maguire), 32 (© Santamaradona); Getty Images: pp. 8 (Apic/Hulton Archive), 9 (SuperStock), 10 (Keystone-France/Gamma-Keystone), 22 (Pascal Le Segretain), 23 (Farouk Batiche/AFP), 28 (© 2009 PKG Photography), 29 (Fayez Nureldine/AFP); iStockphoto: pp. 13 (Michel Gunther), 16 (Jean-Paul Garcin), 18 (Alain Dragesco-Joffé), 21 (Michel Gunther); Shutterstock: pp. 5 (© 46 (© margusson).

Cover photograph of sand dunes in Tassili n'Ajjer, Tuareg, Algeria, reproduced with permission from Photolibrary (Ismadl Schwartz).

We would like to thank Shiera S. el-Malik for her invaluable help in the preparation of this book.

Every effort has been made to contact copyright holders of material reproduced in this book. Any omissions will be rectified in subsequent printings if notice is given to the publisher.

Disclaimer
All the internet addresses (URLs) given in this book were valid at the time of going to press. However, due to the dynamic nature of the internet, some addresses may have changed, or sites may have changed or ceased to exist since publication. While the author and publisher regret any inconvenience this may cause readers, no responsibility for any such changes can be accepted by either the author or the publisher.

ROTHERHAM LIBRARY SERVICE	
B53045339	
Bertrams	08/03/2013
JN	£8.99
CLS	J965.054

It is easy to get lost in Algeria. The Sahara Desert covers much of the country. The Sahara, the world's largest desert, covers 8.6 million square kilometres (3.3 million square miles) of Africa.

History: struggle for independence and peace

Algeria's long history is marked by invasions. As a result, its boundaries have changed many times. Algeria finally gained **independence** in 1962. For the last 50 years, the country has experienced **unrest** because of conflicts over government and religion.

The original people

The first **inhabitants** in the region of Algeria were called **Berbers**. The Berbers were herders and hunters. Over time, the Sahara Desert expanded over the grassy herding areas. The Berbers gradually moved north to the mountains and coastal region near the Mediterranean Sea.

Ancient conquerors

Around 1100 BC, the first non-Berber people settled in North Africa. These people came from Phoenicia, an ancient land now known as Lebanon. The Phoenicians **subdued** the Berbers, taking many of them as slaves. The conquerors built towns along the coast so they could **trade** goods with others by way of the sea.

In the 800s BC, the Algerian region came under the control of Carthage, an ancient trading city. Many Berbers were trained to fight in the Carthaginian army. Over the next 600 years, the Berbers sometimes fought for Carthage and sometimes fought for another empire based in the city of Rome.

Rome defeated Carthage and took over North Africa in 105 BC. The Romans established farms that produced grains, grapes, beans, and olive oil. The Romans also brought Christianity to the region. Christianity became the religion of about 30 per cent of the people.

The ancient Romans built roads and aqueducts in the lands they invaded. Remains of these structures still exist in Algeria.

Some Berbers stayed in the mountain regions of Algeria through the invasions. These Berbers preserved a unique, ancient language and culture.

More invasions and the arrival of Islam

Over time, the Roman Empire weakened. The Vandals, a fierce tribe from Germany, invaded Roman-occupied North Africa in AD 429. Troops from the Byzantine Empire then defeated the Vandals in AD 534.

In the 600s, **Arab** armies invaded North Africa. The Arabs brought the religion of **Islam** with them. Over the next 600 years, most Berbers adopted Islam and the Arab culture. Berbers and Arabs often married each other. Arabic became the shared language across North Africa.

The Ottoman Empire

In the early 1500s, Christian troops from Spain captured Algeria's coastal cities. The Berber rulers feared that their Islamic way of life would end. They asked for help from the **Muslim** Ottoman Empire. The Ottomans, based in present-day Turkey, pushed the Spanish Christians out of North Africa.

As a result, Ottoman governors called *deys* ruled Algeria from the 1500s to the early 1800s. The *deys* allowed the Berber tribes in the mountains to govern themselves. They also allowed North African pirates to attack and demand money from European traders in the Mediterranean Sea. The pirates gave a portion of their money to the *deys*.

In 1529, Khayr al-Din led the capture of Algiers for the Ottoman Empire. Europeans nicknamed him "Barbarossa," which means "red beard" in Italian.

EL-HADJI-ABD-EL-KADER.

French invasion

The pirates' reign ended in 1830 when France invaded the city of Algiers. The French then expanded their power to the mountain areas. In 1848, Algeria officially became a part of France, and Algeria's modern borders were established.

Guided by Muslim leader Abd al-Qadir, many Arabs and Berbers fought fiercely against French control.

Colonial rule

France encouraged Europeans to move to Algeria. The Europeans received free or low-cost land to farm. Often, Muslim families had to move to cities or less **fertile** land as a result. Under French rule, Muslim Algerians could not serve in the government or even vote.

Struggle for independence

In 1954, the Algerian National Liberation Front (FLN) started a violent **revolt** against the French government. The French fought back by burning homes and farms. After eight years of fighting, Algeria declared independence from France on 5 July 1962.

In a demonstration for independence, Algerians confront the French army.

Internal struggles

The new government made decisions that helped a few, but not all, Algerians. Many Algerians remained poor. By the mid-1980s, many Algerians were angry with the government. **Riots** broke out across the country in 1988.

In response, the government allowed more than one **political party** to take part in elections. The Islamic Salvation Front (FIS) wanted to make Algeria a country ruled by **sharia**, or laws based on the Muslim holy book, the **Koran**. To stop this from happening, the military took action.

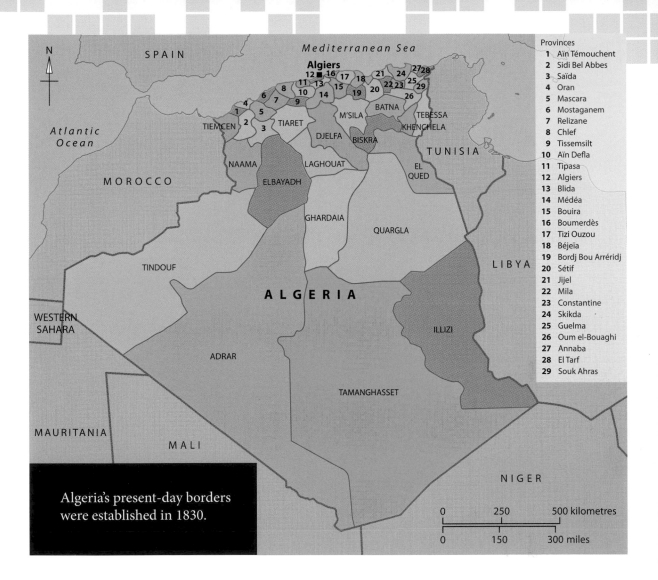

N

SPAIN

Mediterranean Sea

Algiers

12 ■ 16 17 21 24 27 28
11 13 18 22 23 25 29
4 6 8 10 14 15 19 20 26
1 5 7 9
TIEMCEN 2 3 TIARET M'SILA BATNA TEBESSA KHENCHELA

Atlantic Ocean

DJELFA BISKRA

NAAMA LAGHOUAT EL QUED TUNISIA

MOROCCO ELBAYADH

GHARDAIA

QUARGLA LIBYA

TINDOUF

ALGERIA

ILLIZI

WESTERN SAHARA

ADRAR

TAMANGHASSET

MAURITANIA

MALI

NIGER

Provinces

1	Aïn Témouchent
2	Sidi Bel Abbes
3	Saïda
4	Oran
5	Mascara
6	Mostaganem
7	Relizane
8	Chlef
9	Tissemsilt
10	Aïn Defla
11	Tipasa
12	Algiers
13	Blida
14	Médéa
15	Bouira
16	Boumerdès
17	Tizi Ouzou
18	Béjeïa
19	Bordj Bou Arréridj
20	Sétif
21	Jijel
22	Mila
23	Constantine
24	Skikda
25	Guelma
26	Oum el-Bouaghi
27	Annaba
28	El Tarf
29	Souk Ahras

Algeria's present-day borders were established in 1830.

0   250   500 kilometres

0   150   300 miles

A seven-year civil war erupted between the military-backed government and the FIS. Factories, bridges, railways, and other buildings were purposefully damaged during the war. An estimated 100,000 people died.

In 1999, with the support of the military, Abdelaziz Bouteflika was **elected** president. Violence decreased as a result of Bouteflika's effort to work with the **mullahs**, the Muslim religious leaders. However, recent **protests** produced conflicts with police and showed that some Algerians remain angry with the government.

Regions and resources: mostly desert

Algeria is situated in northern Africa along the Mediterranean Sea. It is one of the largest countries in Africa. The Tellian Atlas Mountains and the Saharan Atlas Mountains cross Algeria from east to west. These mountain ranges divide the country into three zones, or regions.

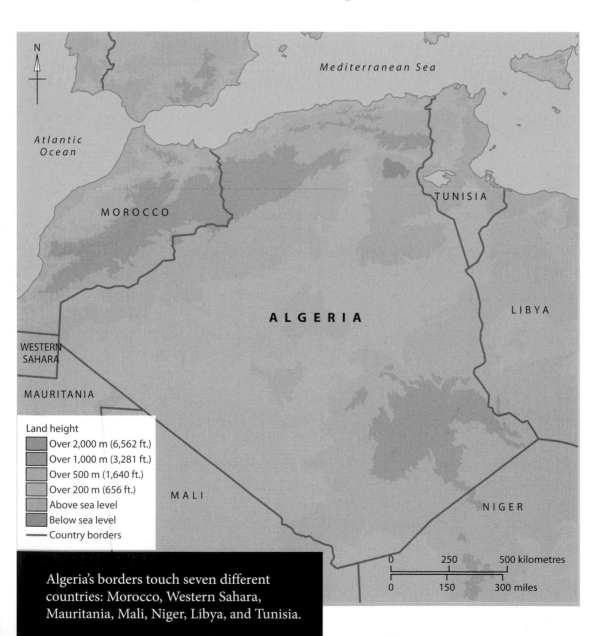

N

Mediterranean Sea

Atlantic Ocean

MOROCCO

TUNISIA

LIBYA

A L G E R I A

WESTERN SAHARA

MAURITANIA

Land height
- Over 2,000 m (6,562 ft.)
- Over 1,000 m (3,281 ft.)
- Over 500 m (1,640 ft.)
- Over 200 m (656 ft.)
- Above sea level
- Below sea level
- Country borders

MALI

NIGER

| 0 | 250 | 500 kilometres |
| 0 | 150 | 300 miles |

Algeria's borders touch seven different countries: Morocco, Western Sahara, Mauritania, Mali, Niger, Libya, and Tunisia.

Algeria's northern border spans the Mediterranean Sea. The coastline is beautiful, but rough.

The coastal zone

Between the Tellian Atlas Mountains and the Mediterranean Sea lies a narrow, hilly coastal zone. The land here is **fertile**. The mild climate makes this region, called the Tell (the Algerian word for "hill"), good for **agriculture**. Summers are hot and dry; winters are mild and wet. Algeria's few rivers twist among these hills and valleys.

The Tell is home to 90 per cent of the Algerian population. Major cities such as Algiers, Oran, and Constantine are scattered along the Mediterranean coast. Severe earthquakes shake this region regularly. Floods and mudslides can also present problems during the rainy winters.

Daily life

In the spring and summer, a hot, dry wind called the **sirocco** blows north across the Sahara Desert. The wind picks up sand as it travels. When it reaches the coastal region, the sirocco coats everything with a thin film of dust. The dust can make it difficult to breathe. Most Algerians wear scarves to protect their faces. When the sirocco is blowing, it can be difficult to see more than 30 metres (100 feet) ahead.

High plateaus

Between the Tellian Atlas and Saharan Atlas mountain ranges is a high **plateau** region. This area averages an elevation (height) of 914 metres (3,000 feet) above sea level. With limited rainfall and high winds, the land is dry and rough. Still, the plateaus are home to over 3 million Algerians. These Algerians farm sheep, cattle, goats, and barley to survive.

The Sahara Desert

South of the Saharan Atlas Mountains, the Sahara Desert covers the rest of Algeria. The temperature here during the day can reach 49ºC (120ºF) and then drop to near freezing at night. Certain sections of the desert go without rain for up to 20 years. The sand dunes are usually between 2 and 5 metres (7 and 16 feet) high, but some are taller than palm trees!

Although the Sahara Desert takes up 80 per cent of Algeria's land, only 3 per cent of the population lives here. Most of these 1.5 million people are **nomads** or semi-settled **Bedouin**, desert-dwelling **Arab** tribes. However, some Algerians live permanently in **oases** where water from beneath the ground reaches the surface.

Daily life

The Tuareg Berbers have made their home in the Sahara Desert for thousands of years. Today, Tuaregs trade camels, breed cattle, and create objects from metal. They produce beautiful swords, jewellery, and metal crafts. When travelling by camel, Tuaregs use saddles that make the ride more comfortable and also provide storage space.

The Sahara Desert contains more than just sand. Rock cliffs, large stones, and gravel are found at Mount Tahat, Algeria's highest point.

Oil **refineries** and pipelines are common in Algeria's desert.

Natural energy resources

Algeria's desert is not a welcoming place to live. However, large **reserves** of oil and natural gas lie under the ground. Oil was first discovered in Algeria in 1956. Since that time, the oil and gas **industries** have provided wealth for Algeria. More than 95 per cent of money earned through **exporting** comes from these **resources**.

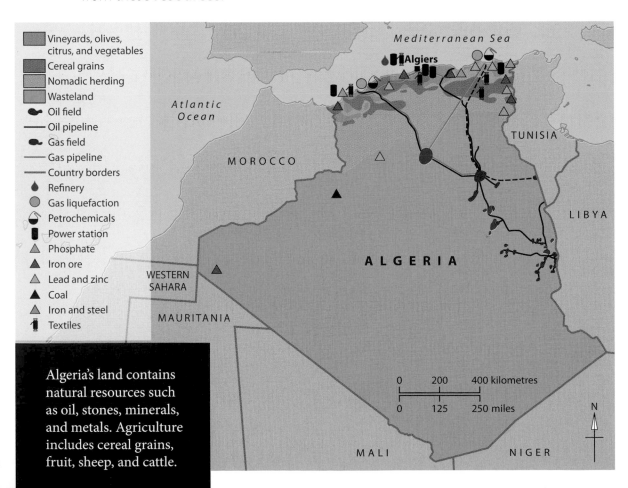

Key
- Vineyards, olives, citrus, and vegetables
- Cereal grains
- Nomadic herding
- Wasteland
- Oil field
- Oil pipeline
- Gas field
- Gas pipeline
- Country borders
- Refinery
- Gas liquefaction
- Petrochemicals
- Power station
- Phosphate
- Iron ore
- Lead and zinc
- Coal
- Iron and steel
- Textiles

Algeria's land contains natural resources such as oil, stones, minerals, and metals. Agriculture includes cereal grains, fruit, sheep, and cattle.

The mining industry

Besides oil and gas, Algeria has other important resources under the ground. Minerals such as iron, lead, zinc, and copper are continually **mined** from Algerian land. Phosphate, a mineral used in fertilizer, has been mined since 1891. Algerians also mine salt, gold, cement, and valuable stones such as **onyx** and marble.

Factories and farms

Manufacturing is another important industry in Algeria. The most common products made in the factories are steel, **textiles**, and construction materials. Factories also process food and electricity.

Agriculture provides jobs for 14 per cent of the Algerian population. Most farms are located in the Tell where the soil is **fertile**. Algerians grow cereal grains such as rye, wheat, barley, and oats. Fruits such as figs, grapes, citrus, and olives are also common crops. Sheep are reared for their wool and meat, while cattle are bred for dairy products and meat.

The government provides almost one-third of the jobs in Algeria. This chart shows the division of labour in Algeria.

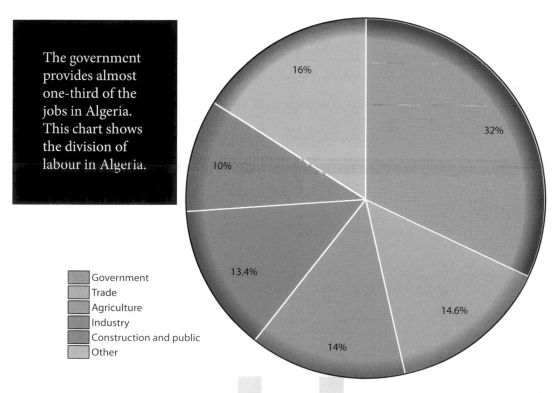

16%

32%

10%

13.4%

14%

14.6%

Government
Trade
Agriculture
Industry
Construction and public
Other

National parks

Algeria has many national parks. The land and animals in these parks are protected so that Algerians can enjoy them both now and in the future. The parks cover a variety of **ecosystems**, including the coast, desert, and mountains.

Gouraya National Park has beautiful beaches as well as tall cliffs. The park includes the waters of the Mediterranean Sea near the coast. Marine mammals such as the harbour porpoise, bottlenose dolphin, and sperm whale find protection here.

Djurdjura National Park is located in a mountainous region in northern Algeria. This area is known for its thick forests, unusual caves, and beautiful lakes. The park is home to a variety of animals, including the red fox, weasel, and peregrine falcon. The endangered Barbary macque, a type of monkey, also lives in Djurdjura National Park.

Tassili n'Ajjer National Park contains sandstone cliffs and arches. Scientists believe rock paintings in the park are 7,000 years old.

Water pollution

Many Algerians want to keep their land and water clean. However, some **industries** dump **sewage** and oil waste into rivers and the Mediterranean Sea. Soil and fertilizer from farms also wash into the waterways. Many Algerian people and animals do not have clean water to drink.

Chemicals and waste collect in rivers and streams in Algeria. The pollution makes the water unsafe to drink.

How to say...

Arabic, the official language of Algeria, is written with an alphabet different from the Roman alphabet. The Arabic words below have been written with the Roman alphabet so that you can pronounce them.

falcon	*ajdal*	**desert**	*badiya*
forest	*haraj*	**cave**	*ghar*
monkey	*hibn*	**mountain**	*jabal*
whale	*hut*	**sea**	*bakhr*

Education

Algerians value education. The education system has grown tremendously since the country's **independence** in 1962. Before independence, fewer than 10 per cent of Algerians could read and write. Now the **literacy rate** is about 70 per cent.

Literacy rates	
Female	60.1%
Male	79.6%
Total population	69.9%

Algeria provides free education to all children. Schooling is required for nine years, from age 6 to 16. Pupils must pass a national exam to get into secondary school. They also compete against each other for places at universities or technical colleges.

Because the majority of Algerians are under the age of 20, schools tend to be crowded. In some cities, children go to school in shifts – one group in the morning, and a different group in the afternoon.

Algerian primary school children learn maths, Arabic, history, science, and the fundamentals of **Islam**. Some study French, starting in Year 4. Children learn to write both the Roman alphabet as well as the traditional, flowing Arabic script.

How to say...

book	*kitab*	**student**	*daris*
school	*madrasa*	**mathematics**	*rayadi*
history	*tarikh*	**university**	*jami'a*

YOUNG PEOPLE

Algerian children do not have to wear
a uniform in school. In fact, they often
wear comfortable clothing such as jeans
and T-shirts. However, pupils must dress
modestly. Lunch is eaten at school. The
government provides a school lunch for
children of families with little money.

Algerian children attend
school for about six hours
per day. The school day starts
around 8.00 a.m.

Urban life

Over half of all Algerians now live in urban areas. Many **rural** families move to cities in search of work, but there are not enough jobs for everyone. There are not enough places to live, either. Algeria is currently short of 1.5 million homes, even after large construction projects in the 1990s.

Slums have developed on the outskirts of Algeria's cities as a result of housing shortages and unemployment. These neighbourhoods are overcrowded, run-down, and often dirty and unhealthy. Some of these areas lack basic services such as clean drinking water, electricity, or waste disposal.

Population of major cities in Algeria	
Algiers	2,900,000
Oran	1,170,000
Constantine	808,000
Annaba	350,000

Healthcare

The Algerian government provides free basic medical care through a system of clinics and hospitals. Algerians enjoy better health conditions than most people in Africa. Still, the number of doctors, nurses, and dentists is small compared to the number of Algerians who need healthcare.

Currency

The dinar is the official **currency** in Algeria. Dinars were introduced in 1964 after independence from France. Algerians use dinars in the form of coins and bills.

Pictures of important buildings, animals, and locations are printed on Algerian money.

Many Algerians live in apartment blocks. It is typical for nine people to live together in a three-bedroomed apartment.

Daily life

Algerians who need to travel within the country usually drive cars or trucks. Most of the major roads are paved, except in the southern Sahara region. Some people who live in the desert still travel by camel.

Culture: life together

Algerians are proud of their land and culture. Traditions are important, and family is the foundation of society. Many Algerians express their identities and feelings through art, including literature and music.

The people

Ninety-nine per cent of Algerians are **Arab**, **Berber**, or mixed Arab-Berber. Sometimes Berbers and Arabs clash because of differences in language and power in government.

Arabic is the official language of Algeria. However, Berbers speak Tamazight, a language that was recognized by the government only in 2002. French is widely understood in Algeria and used in media, education, and government.

Daily life

Algerian men often gather at coffee shops or cafés to play chess, draughts, cards, or dominoes. Although women sometimes join them, they are more likely to socialize at home.

Muslim prayers are said five times daily.

After Algeria's independence, more women began to attend university and take professional jobs. These women are newly graduated police officers.

Religion

Both Berbers and Arabs follow **Islam**, Algeria's main religion. Followers of Islam are called **Muslims**, and the vast majority of Algerians are **Sunni** Muslims. Muslims believe their holy book, the **Koran**, contains the words of God as told to the Prophet Muhammad.

Role of women

Typically, an Algerian woman marries the man her father chooses for her. In traditional families, women rarely have jobs outside the home. Most Algerian women cover their faces in public, according to traditional Islamic custom.

During the war for **independence**, some Algerian women actively fought alongside the men. Since then, more and more women have enrolled at universities and colleges and obtained jobs. Today, 60 per cent of university students are women.

Sports

Football is the most popular sport in Algeria. Across the country, people play football in stadiums, empty fields, and school grounds. Algerians also enjoy boxing, wrestling, tennis, running, swimming, and skiing. In the desert areas, camel racing is a favourite sport.

Football is played all over Algeria.

Media

Satellite television is popular in Algeria. Many watch both European and Arab channels. Algerians have access to a variety of newspapers and radio stations. The government controls most media sources, yet there is more freedom of speech than in other North African countries.

Algeria's major cities have internet access. In 2008, 4.1 million Algerians were using the internet, mostly in cybercafés or with dial-up connections. Mobile phones are now quite common, especially amongst young people.

Food

Algerians enjoy meals with family and friends. The traditional Arabic flatbread, called *khabz*, is an Algerian **staple**. Algerians eat lamb, beef, and fish. Meals usually include vegetables and are flavoured with dried red chilies, black pepper, cumin, and other spices.

Coclo (Big Meatballs)

Coclo is enjoyed by many Algerians. Ask an adult to help you make this recipe.

Ingredients

- 450 g minced beef
- 140 g rice
- 1 clove of garlic, finely chopped
- 1 medium egg, beaten
- ½ teaspoon salt
- ½ teaspoon ground bayleaf
- ⅛ teaspoon ground mace
- ¼ teaspoon pepper
- ⅛ teaspoon thyme
- 2 tablespoons olive oil
- 1 medium onion, finely chopped
- ½ bunch of coriander leaves, tied in a bundle
- 175 ml water

Method

1. Mix the beef, rice, garlic, egg, salt, bay leaf, mace, pepper, thyme, and olive oil together well. Shape into two large meatballs.
2. Put onion, coriander, and water in a pan. Add meatballs. Cover the pan and simmer over low heat for 2 hours or a bit more.
3. Discard the coriander. Serve the meatballs with rice or couscous.

Serves 6

Algeria today

After years of turmoil and violence, Algeria is making strides toward peace and **stability**. In the last 50 years, the **economy** has benefited from oil and gas discoveries. Now all Algerian children have access to school. Security in the cities has improved through active police presence and safety measures.

Yet Algeria's cities remain overcrowded, with too many people and too few jobs. In early 2011, **protests** broke out in Algeria over **unemployment** and the high prices of food. Two people were killed in conflicts with police. In response, the government promised changes to improve the economy. Some Algerians question the government's ability or honest desire to help the common people.

Militant Islamic groups have also increased public attacks and bombings since 2006. These groups do not want the Algerian government to join with other countries to fight **terrorism**. Instead, they want the Algerian government to be led more strongly by **sharia**.

Despite the continuing conflicts, Algerians remain committed to their families, their culture, and their beliefs. Algerians are known to be warm and welcoming to friends and neighbours. They enjoy sharing food, sports and games, and lively conversation.

The strong people and natural **resources** of Algeria provide the building blocks for a stable nation. With more pubic services, job opportunities, and honesty in government, Algerians can look forward to a good future in their beautiful, rugged land.

Algerians are very hospitable. A popular Algerian saying expresses this kindness toward visitors: "When you come to our house, it is we who are the guests, for this is your house."

Natural resources:	petroleum, natural gas, iron ore, phosphates, uranium, lead, zinc
Industries:	petroleum, natural gas, light industries, mining, electrical, petrochemical, food processing
Agricultural products:	wheat, barley, oats, grapes, olives, citrus, fruit, sheep, cattle

National holidays:

1 January	New Year's Day
1 May	Labour Day
19 June	National Day
5 July	Independence Day
1 November	Anniversary of the Revolution

Famous Algerians:

St Augustine (AD 354–430), writer and philosopher

Abdelkader Alloula (1929–1994), playwright

Ahmed Ben Bella (b. 1918), Algeria's first president

Hassiba Boulmerka (b. 1968), Olympic runner

Albert Camus (1913–1960), writer

Sidi Bu Madyan (1126–1198), Islamic mystic, Algeria's patron saint

Hamid Cheriet (b. 1949), musician

Cheb Mami (b. 1966), singer

Abd al-Qadir (1808–1883), resistance fighter against the French

Workers on farms make up 14 per cent of the work force in Algeria.

Topic tools

You can use these topic tools for your school projects. Trace the map on to a sheet of paper, using the thick black outline to guide you.

The Algerian flag is half green and half white. The colour green represents Islam. The colour white stands for purity and peace. The red crescent and star in the middle are symbols of Islam. The colour red represents liberty.

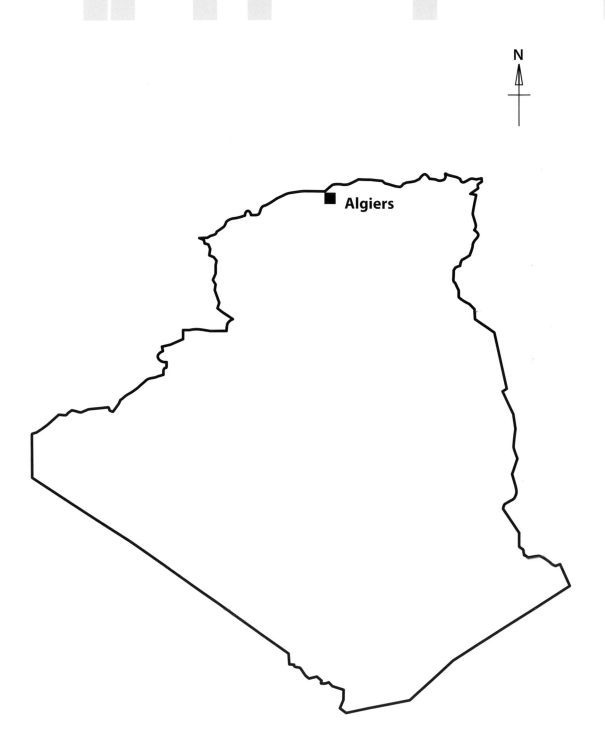

Algiers

N

Index